images
of greatness

images of

greatness
– a celebration of life

compiled and illustrated by
David Melton

Published by
LANDMARK EDITIONS, INC.
1402 Kansas Avenue • Kansas City, Missouri 64127 • (816) 241-4919
In Association with
THE INTERNATIONAL IMAGES OF GREATNESS COMMISSION
11009 E. 85th Street • Kansas City, Missouri 64138

To Nancy

Second Printing

Revised Edition

Published by
LANDMARK EDITIONS, INC.
1402 Kansas Avenue
Kansas City, Missouri 64127
(816) 241-4919

In Association with
THE INTERNATIONAL IMAGES OF GREATNESS
COMMISSION
11009 E. 85th Street
Kansas City, Missouri 64138

ISBN: 0-933849-11-7

Library of Congress Cataloging-in-Publication Data

Images of greatness.

   Summary: Illustrations and quotations of notable world citizens emphasize the pos-
sibilities of continued service and creativity through old age.
   1. Life—Quotations, maxims, etc. 2. Old age—Quotations, maxims, etc. [1. Old
age—Quotations, maxims, etc.] I. Melton, David.
PN6084.L53I4   1987   082   87-26300
ISBN 0-933849-11-7

images of greatness Registered Trademark

Book Design by David Melton

Editorial Coordinator, Nancy R. Thatch

Printed in the United States of America

Will Geer

Colonel Harland Sanders

Maggie Kuhn

Congressman Claude Pepper

Viewers enjoy "Images of Greatness" Exhibit.

Leroy "Satchel" Paige

Introduction

In an effort to improve public attitudes toward the elderly, THE INTERNATIONAL IMAGES OF GREATNESS COMMISSION, in 1975, sought a way to remind society that older people have made and continue to make major contributions to the world. To achieve our objective, we chose a simple, but most elegant idea — we commissioned renowned artist/author David Melton to create a series of large pencil illustrations which could be exhibited throughout the country.

At a ceremony on November 23, 1975, the first illustrations, entitled IMAGES OF GREATNESS, were unveiled at Swope Ridge Health Care Center in Kansas City, Missouri. A limited number of 350 sets of full-sized reproductions were sent to select persons and organizations. Within months exhibits were opened at: Notre Dame University; The National Headquarters Building of the Medicare Bureau, Washington, D.C.; The Institutes for the Achievement of Human Potential, Philadelphia, Pennsylvania; The Harry S. Truman Library and Museum, Independence, Missouri; and in numerous universities, libraries and health care centers throughout the nation.

What began as gentle reminders became awards for lifetimes of achievement and service. THE IMAGES OF GREAT-NESS AWARDS have been ceremoniously or personally presented to many persons represented in this book. Posthumous awards have also been presented to members of the honorees' families and/or were made public.

While turning the pages of this wonderful book, we are reminded that old age does not mean old ideas and that gray hair does not signal the end to activity and personal involvement. Wherever we look, we find men and women, past the ages of 65, 75 and even 85, who are making important contributions to our society. They are active in every endeavor. They are visible in business, government and the arts. They are valued in the sciences, and in religion, journalism and sports. They are found in world, national and community affairs.

Margaret Mead, Igor Stravinsky, Thomas A. Edison, Harry S. Truman, Albert Schweitzer, Helen Hayes, Pablo Picasso, Albert Einstein, Louis "Satchmo" Armstrong, and many others are featured in this extraordinary book, compiled and illustrated by artist/author David Melton.

As always, Mr. Melton's selectivity and versatility are wonders to behold. His pencil provides visual delights. His style is boldly dramatic, his approach unique. He deftly reveals the personalities of his subjects without hesitating to enlist the imagination of the viewer. And the selection of featured quotations reflects his high regard for older people, not as mere members of a group, but as individuals in their own right.

I hope you and your family will be as inspired and challenged by IMAGES OF GREATNESS as my family and I have been. It is truly a book for everyone to enjoy.

—Barry L. Seward

Chairman
THE INTERNATIONAL
IMAGES OF GREATNESS COMMISSION

images of greatness

Winter is on my head, but eternal spring is in my heart. I breathe at this hour the fragrance of the lilacs, the violets and the roses, as at twenty years.

—Victor Hugo

Youth is not a time of life—it is a state of mind.... Nobody grows old by merely living a number of years; people grow old only by deserting their ideals. Years wrinkle the skin, but to give up enthusiasm wrinkles the soul. Worry, doubt, self-distrust, fear, and despair—these are the long, long years that bow the head and turn the growing spirit back to the dust.

Whether seventy or sixteen, there is in every being's heart the love of wonder, the sweet amazement at the stars and the starlike things and thoughts, the undaunted challenge of events, the unfailing childlike appetite for what next, and the joy and the game of life.

You are as young as your faith, as old as your doubt; as young as your self-confidence, as old as your fear; as young as your hope, as old as your despair.

—Samuel Ullman

Only a life lived for others is a life worth while.

—Albert Einstein

Two things are bad for the heart —
running up stairs and running down people.

—Bernard M. Baruch

DAVID MELTON

I feel reborn each day. First I go to nature. It is a rediscovery of the world in which I have the joy of being a part. It fills me with the awareness of the wonder of life, with a feeling of incredible marvel of being a human being. Then I go to the piano and I play two preludes and fugues of Bach. It is a sort of benediction of the house. The music is never the same to me; each day is something new, fantastic, unbelievable.

—Pablo Casals

Play with your hearts, not your instruments!

—Arturo Toscanini

...is dissent necessary? You're damned right. We have a country that could be heaven on earth, but instead it has unnecessary poverty, discrimination against the black and the poor, and the continuous possibility of nuclear warfare....Everything that is wrong about the world is caused by a lack of moral conviction and moral initiative. For the moralist there is always evil in the universe to be combated.

—Benjamin Spock, M.D.

I had much to learn, and at eighty, I found new vistas opening all around me.

The riders in a race do not stop short when they reach the goal. There is a little finishing canter before coming to a standstill. There is time to hear the kind voice of friends and to say to one's self: "The work is done." But just as one says that, the answer comes: "The race is over, but the work never is done while the power to work remains." The canter that brings you to a standstill need not be only coming to rest. It cannot be, while you still live. For to live is to function. That is all there is in living.

—Oliver Wendell Holmes

Look to this day!
For it is life, the very life of life....
For yesterday is already a dream, and tomorrow
  is only a vision;
But today, well lived, makes every yesterday
A dream of happiness, and every tomorrow a
  vision of hope.

—From the Sanskrit

*Life was meant to be lived, and curiosity must be
    kept alive.
  One must never, for whatever reason, turn his
    back on life.*

—Eleanor Roosevelt

Would you fashion for yourself a seemly life?
Then do not fret over what is past and gone;
In spite of all you may have left behind
Live each day as if your life had just begun.

—J. W. von Goethe

If human life were motivated solely by economic considerations, there would be no point in discussing freedom and still less in dying for it.

—Evan W. Thomas, M.D.

Life is not easy for any of us. But what of that? We must have perseverence and above all confidence in ourselves. We must believe we are gifted for something, and that this thing, at whatever cost, must be attained.

—Marie Curie

. . ."retire" is the wrong word. You can't retire what God gave you. I still sing better than ever. But I'm more of a philosopher than a singer, and what better time to leave than when I have something to give?

—Pearl Bailey

Let us cherish and love old age; for it is full of pleasure, if one knows how to use it.

—Seneca

AGING PAYS

Chemicals in the human body, valued at about 98 cents in the 1930's, are worth about $800 today.—News item.

I get up early every morning. I'm at work by eight. I still play a fair game of badminton. I no longer believe that I'll bring back the golden age of illustration. I realized a long time ago that I'll never be as good as Rembrandt. But I think my work is improving. I start each picture with the same high hopes, and if I never seem able to fulfill them I still try my darnedest.

—Norman Rockwell

. . .my life is more thrilling today than it ever was. I am in good health and still creative and have plans to produce more pictures.

—Sir Charles Chaplin

A long life may not be good enough, but a good life is long enough.

—Benjamin Franklin

. . . hardening of arteries is not necessarily associated with hardening of mind. I am exhilarated to discover that I am even more receptive to new ideas than I was as a young man.

—Edward B. LeWinn, M.D.

Speaking only for myself, I not only *hear* music; I *listen* to it when it is around, so that I find Muzak and other background music, intended to be heard but not listened to, utterly intolerable. When I am, in Carl Rogers' terms, open to my experience, I find the colors of the day, whether gray and foggy and muted or bright and sunlit, such vivid experiences that I sometimes pound my steering wheel with excitement. A neon-lit supermarket is often too much for me—so terribly rich in angles and colors and dizzying perspectives that I must deliberately narrow my perceptions to the things on my grocery list lest I take forever to do the shopping. Paintings and sculptures and ceramics get me so intensely excited that I often come out of a museum higher than a kite. In short, I *use* my senses—at least some of them, some of the time.

—S. I. Hayakawa

The generation gap has been widened by America's cultural approach to the aged: grandmother's house with its myriad lessons becomes granny's condominium with vinyl furniture. . . . A young person sees his own future as he observes his grandparents, and he sees his own past too, which is another word for a people's history. Continuity is the message of optimism civilization offers its discontents.

—Margaret Mead

A good man doubles the length
    of his existence;
  to have lived so as to look back
    with pleasure
on our past life is to live twice.

—Marcus Valerius Martialis

I am an optimist.
It does not seem too much use being anything else.

—Sir Winston Churchill

Surely the vital thing in old age is to maintain an interest and never stop planning for the future. I started painting at sixty and am still intensely caught up in it. I am studying classical guitar and I've also just taken up the bugle, trying to learn all the traditional carriage calls. For my physical well-being, I still put on a record and do a chorus or two of buck dancing. It's a mistake to set limits on yourself; life will do that whether you like it or not. A successful life must be determined by one's attitude. In a favorite phrase of my brother, Ed, ''We live between our ears.'' Sermon over.

—James Cagney

Where is music is a church!

—Arturo Toscanini

The eye which is called the window of the soul is the chief means whereby the understanding may most fully and abundantly appreciate the infinite works of nature; and the ear is the second inasmuch as it acquires its importance from the face that it hears the things which the eye has seen. If you historians, poets, or mathematicians have never seen things with your eyes you would be ill able to describe them in your writings.

— Leonardo da Vinci

The goal of life is imminent in each
    moment, each thought, word, act,
and does not have to be sought apart
    from these.

—S. E. Stanton

Since courage is better than fear, and faith is better than doubt, let us spurn fear, cherish faith, and dedicate ourselves to this proposition: Freedom is life's supreme value and must be preserved for ourselves and our posterity, cost what it may.
— Senator Sam Ervin

I have only one desire left: never to lose the feeling that it is I who am indebted for what has been given to me from the time that I first learned about Zionism in a small room in Czarist Russia all the way through to my half century, here, where I have seen my five grandchildren grow up as free Jews in a country that is our own. Let no one anywhere have any doubts about this. Our children's children will never settle for anything less.

—Golda Meir

If you have to ask what jazz is, you'll never know.
—Louis ''Satchmo'' Armstrong

No race can prosper till it learns that there is as much dignity in tilling a field as in writing a poem.

—Booker T. Washington

As long as they keep wanting to hear these rusty old pipes, I guess I'll keep right on singing.

—Bing Crosby

Life does not begin and end; it is a cycle. Birth, maturity, death and rebirth, the seasons, the paths of the stars—all these things change, but nothing is added and nothing is taken away. There is no creation; whatever is, always was. In constant mutation, going through millions of permutations and combinations, in perpetual transformation, and yet not adding or subtracting one atom: everything is subject to the same law. If God created the world, who created Him? And on this subject I am wont to quote a little Bible to back me up. "In the beginning was the Word, and the Word was with God...in Him was life, and the life was the light of men." In the beginning was God's law—the law of nature, if you will. It always existed, and it is what controls life and us.

—George Abbott

...my father used to say something from *Hamlet*, "There's a divinity that shapes our ends, rough-hew them how we will," and this quotation has been a controlling factor all through my life.

—Temple Fay, M.D.

It's easier, you know, to become a critic of writing or painting than of music. Everyone can read or look at a painting but few of the music critics can read music properly.

—Igor Stravinsky

...I have an eternal curiosity....
I love people, I love my family, my children....
But inside myself is a place where I live all alone and that's where you renew your springs that never dry up.

—Pearl S. Buck

Silence is deep as Eternity,
Speech is shallow as Time.

—Thomas Carlyle

In one's creative hands rests the greatest mental stabilizer known to man.

—Edward T. Hall

I believe in living for the living. You can't go around feeling sorry for yourself. I'm naturally a cheerful person. My father used to call me Mary Sunshine. I've never told anybody that before.

—Mamie Eisenhower

When grace is joined with wrinkles, it is adorable. There is an unspeakable dawn in happy old age.

—Victor Hugo

My favorite text in the Bible is John 10:10: "I have come that ye might have life and have it more abundantly." As we go from childhood on into older age we should continue to explore the fullness of this abundance., Anyone who says, "I've had my best days, I'm now moving into the sunset"—why that's preposterous talk.

—Dr. Norman Vincent Peale

Let me grow lovely, growing old—
So many fine things do:
Laces and ivory, and gold,
    And silks need not be new.

—Karle Wilson Baker

When practiced by the artist, photography becomes a medium capable of giving form to ideas and incisive expression to a wide range of emotions and concepts. . . . The swift freezing of an exact instant; the gamut of feeling written on the human face in its contrasts of joy, serenity or despair; the beauty of the earth that man has inherited and the wealth and the confusion of the earth that man has created within this inheritance—these are often rendered with a sense of timelessness and exactitude.

Every day of life *is* a beautiful day.

—Edward Steichen

When I was a boy of fourteen, my father was so ignorant I could hardly stand to have the old man around. But when I got to be twenty-one, I was astonished at how much he had learned in seven years.

*—Mark Twain
(Samuel L. Clemens)*

What does it mean to grow older?
It means to grow wiser each day...
To appreciate more fully the joy life sends our
    way...
To find pleasure in simple things:
  a word...a smile...a thought...
To plan and dream, but not forget the joys the past
    has brought.

—Eleanor Woods

*No one should postpone the study of philosophy
when he is young, nor should be weary of it when
he becomes mature, because the search for mental
health is never over nor out of season.*

—Epicurus

The main thing about life is to be *involved*. My
father was a philosopher and when he came into the
house he didn't ask, "How are the kids?" or "How's
business?"; he'd be pulling clippings out of his
pockets and saying, "You see the lousy editorial this
guy wrote in the paper? Let's answer him!" He was
involved. It's what the French call l'homme
engagé—the engaged man.

—Harry Golden

Working keeps me young.
        I have something to live for.

—Eubie Blake

Cheerfulness and content are great beautifiers and
are famous preservers of youthful looks.

—Charles Dickens

*Man is capable of achieving anything that his mind
can imagine.*

—Raymond A. Dart, M.D.

*It was our privilege for a little while to serve that
beautiful thing—the film—and we never doubted for
a moment that it was the most powerful thing—the
mind and heartbeat of our technical century....*

—Lillian Gish

Do not squander time, for that is the stuff life is made of.
— Benjamin Franklin

They call me a "playboy," you know. I want to make things that are fun to look at, that have no propaganda value whatsoever.
—Alexander Calder

...the general undervaluation of the human soul is so great that neither the great religions nor the philosophies nor scientific rationalism have been willing to look at it twice.
—Carl G. Jung

I couldn't let my life slip by without having a record of it. I am busier than ever. I am taking more pictures than ever. I love the Grand Canyon. I want to go to California to go surfing. I think surfing is very amusing. Yes, I am finished with being young —but I'm not old. I don't like old people. Very few old people are marvelous. Most are boring and pessimists. I'm an optimist. It's good to exist.
—Jacques Henri Lartigue

I'm opposed to basing any action on one's age. There are many people who are young at 80, younger than those of 40. I think it's very, very bad for people to *have* to retire at a certain age when, with their experience and capability, they should go on and give others the benefit of their backgrounds.
—Margaret Chase Smith

Retire? Are you kidding? I'm having the time of my life. What would I do, go fishing? Fish don't applaud, do they?
—Bob Hope

Man must not limit life to the affirmation of Man alone. Man's ethics must not end with man, but should extend to the universe. He must regain the consciousness of the great chain of life from which he cannot be separated. He must understand that all creation has its value, and requires of man the same reverence one feels so personally toward loved ones. The will to live motivates all life, and life should only be negated when it is for a higher value and purpose—not in merely selfish or thoughtless actions. What then results for man is not only a deepening of relationships, but a widening of relationships. Life, itself, becomes sacred.
—Albert Schweitzer

Just as I wouldn't judge anyone on the basis of sex, race or religion, I wouldn't rely on an arbitrary stereotype such as age. Competency is a far better basis for judging mandatory retirement.

—Ashley Montagu

Conquering fears, whatever they may be, opens life up—and this life should be as full of different experiences as we can make it.... I'll never settle down to my knitting and live with loneliness. There are too damned many exciting things I haven't tried yet. And I'm planning to try quite a few of them!

—Joan Crawford

I know I am unreasonable about people but there are so many wonderful people whom I *can't take the time to know.*

—Georgia O'Keefe

Duty, honor, country.

The shadows are lengthening for me. The twilight is here. My days of old have vanished—tone and tints. They have gone glimmering through the dreams of things that were. Their memory is one of wondrous beauty, watered by tears and coaxed and caressed by the smiles of yesterday.

I listened then, but with thirsty ear, for the witching melody of faint bugles blowing reveille, of far drums beating the long roll.

In my dreams I hear again the crash of guns, the rattle of musketry, the strange, mournful mutter of the battlefield....

—General Douglas MacArthur

If you refuse to accept anything but the best, you very often get it.

—W. Somerset Maugham

...It is still too early for the song of the swan.

—Arthur Fiedler

We must stand up to old age and make up for its drawbacks by taking pains. . . . Nor is it the body only that must be supported, but still more the intellect and the soul, for they are like lamps—unless you feed them with oil, they go out.

—Cicero

I think of man as the most awesome creation in the universe—the word made flesh. If we treat this creation with respect and love—and more important—with understanding of its wonder, we can live long healthy lives.

— Gloria Swanson

If you sit on your duff you're dead. Life is a verb. I just got back from the beach. I ran—jogged, really—a couple of miles. You've got to get out in the air—I think it contributes to the looseness—helps rid the body of some of the poisons we pick up in commercial food.

—Eddie Albert

*You know, when I was a boy in Vitebsk, whenever I wanted to laugh, my mother would put her hand over my mouth and say, "Shah! Shah! Not too loud, or **they** might come and get you." I could never laugh out loud. Now, whenever I hear children shouting and happy, I thank God every day that I can hear such free laughter and rejoice that these children do not feel the hand of fear clutching at their hearts.*

—Marc Chagall

Lord, make me an instrument of Thy
    peace;
Where there is hatred,
    let me sow love.
Where there is injury,
    pardon,
Where there is doubt,
    faith,
Where there is despair,
    hope,
Where there is darkness,
    light,
Where there is sadness,
    joy.

—St. Francis of Assisi

. . . Many have been too thoroughly brainwashed about how age is supposed to make humans act. Those who can do something must understand that people ought to learn and to grow, and to be involved in the lives of others. I am appalled by the number of people who have given up. But, thank heaven, not all of us are willing to become just wrinkled babies.

—Maggie Kuhn

DAVID MELTON

To every thing there is a season,
and a time to every purpose under heaven.

—Ecclesiastes 3:1

Life is the eternal present in the temporal. Life is the *now* event with reaction *past* and resultant *future.*

—R. Buckminster Fuller

When I was a little girl, somebody asked me what I wanted to be and I said, very ungrammatically, "I want a job that I can't see the end of."

—Dame Edith Evans

To see a World in a Grain of Sand
And a Heaven in a Wild Flower
Hold Infinity in the palm of your hand
And Eternity in an hour.

—William Blake

Don't put no constrictions on da people. Leave 'em ta hell alone.

—Jimmy Durante

Mandatory retirement is wrong. As long as a person is healthy and happy, he should not be forced into idleness but encouraged to remain productive.

—Senator Frank Moss

There is a vitality, a life-force, an energy, a quickening that is translated through you into action and because there is only one of you in all of time, this expression is unique. And if you block it, it will never exist through any other medium and be lost. The world will not have it. . . . Keep the channel open.

If I add something to my time, then that is my prize.

—Martha Graham

At first the writers had Grandpa Walton figured for a quiet, mild old duffer who was happy to sit around on a chair. . . but I refused to act old and frail and helpless. When the script suggested I hand my rifle over to John Boy and tell him to go out hunting with it because I was too old, I revolted. I told the directors that as long as I could walk and talk, I'd take my rifle and go up into the mountains to hunt by myself. And I did.

—Will Geer

I am a man of principle, and one of my basic principles is flexibility.

— Senator Everett Dirksen

Every great and commanding moment in the annals of the world is the triumph of some enthusiasm.

— Ralph Waldo Emerson

People of my age are all retiring, which is something I would never want for myself. I'm afraid the average guy enjoys his retirement because he never enjoyed his work. I've got more things I want to do now than ever.

— Ted Geisel (Dr. Seuss)

Bad will be the day for every man when he becomes absolutely content with the life that he is living, with the thoughts that he is thinking, with the deeds that he is doing, when there is not forever beating at the doors of his soul some great desire to do something larger, which he knows that he was meant and made to do, because he is still, in spite of all, the child of God.

— Phillips Brooks

I can tell you from the shade, it was all worthwhile.

— George Jessel

Grow old along with me!
The best is yet to be,
The last of life, for which the first was made.
Our times are in his hand.

— Robert Browning

Think thin! *— Cary Grant*

...life is like a game of tennis. You've got to think ahead. You've got to be aggressive, because if you don't move ahead, you slip behind. Nobody stands still—in a career, in life. So get behind it and shove—that's the way to get it out of the mud—lean forward.

— Katharine Hepburn

Ageism is as odious as racism and sexism. Mandatory retirement arbitrarily severs productive persons from their livelihood, squanders their talent, scars their health, strains an already overburdened Social Security system and drives many elderly persons into poverty and despair.

— Congressman Claude D. Pepper

One advantage in growing older is that you can stand for more and fall for less.

—Monta Crane

George S. Kaufman returned to the Algonquin following a visit to his physician.

"Fool told me I'm going to live to be a hundred," he said gloomily. "Well, I won't."

"How do you know, George?" Edna Ferber asked.

"I'll kill myself at eighty," he told her.

The table grew quiet.

"How?" Miss Ferber asked.

"With kindness," he announced.

Age, like distance, lends a double charm.

—Oliver Wendell Holmes

The young man who has not wept is a savage, and the old man who will not laugh is a fool.

—George Santayana

I've often said I should have been a woman, I'm so easy to persuade.

—Senator Everett Dirksen

I never was a "yes man" and I certainly don't intend to be one now.... In the end I've got to follow my own line of business on the field...you have to give your life to it....I've never been shocked too much, except you should have a hatred for losing...somebody's gotta get them in.

—*Casey Stengel*

Having been so durable myself, I have lived to see our country move through prosperity and depression, war and peace, periods of great national unrest and periods of relative tranquillity. I have seen political thinking swing from right to left and back again. I have reached the age of perspective, and that is one of the heartwarming gifts of time. One is not stampeded or defeated by today's headlines. One knows that beneath the riled surface, there are deep tides and currents, which will eventually prevail.

—*Helen Hayes*

From my childhood I was impelled by a hunger and thirst after divine things—a desire for something higher and better than matter; and apart from it—to seek diligently for the knowledge of God as the one great and ever-present relief from human woe.

—Mary Baker Eddy

I have a cure for boredom that will never fail. It is made up of ten rules: go out among the people and perform one kind act ten times.

—Carrie Chapman Catt

We are all afraid—for our confidence, for the future, for the world. That is the nature of the human imagination. Yet every man, every civilization, has gone forward because of its engagement with what it has set itself to do. The personal commitment of a man to his skill, the intellectual commitment and the emotional commitment working together as one, has made the Ascent of Man.

—J. Bronowski

Do not go gentle into that good night,
Old age should burn and rave at close of day;
  Rage, rage against the dying of the light.

—Dylan Thomas

Genius is one per cent inspiration and ninety-nine per cent perspiration.

—Thomas A. Edison

There's so little time, you see. I feel I've got what, fifteen years if I'm lucky, and so very much left to do. I really couldn't stop now. I enjoy acting today even more than I did during the first twenty years. It's my driving force. In fact, it's my life. I've always worked hard. I've had to force myself to take a holiday when the enthusiasm fails. And that is the hardest part of all.... You see, the only time I ever feel alive is when I'm acting. That sounds a strange paradox, doesn't it....Oh, gosh, that sounds damn silly and pretentious. What I mean is the feeling of being vitally alive when one is actively exploring and creating something new in terms of performance.

—Sir Laurence Olivier

If most of us are ashamed of shabby clothes and shoddy furniture, let us be more ashamed of shabby ideas and shoddy philosophies.

—Albert Einstein

Some measure their lives by days and years,
Others by heart throbs, passion and tears.
But the surest measure under the sun
Is what in your lifetime for others you've done.

—Ruth Smeltzer
from "Truest Measure"

I have often thought that if heaven gave me choice of my position and calling, it should have been on a rich spot of earth, well watered, and near a good market for the production of the garden. No occupation is so delightful to me as the culture of the earth, and no culture comparable to that of the garden. Such a variety of subjects, some one always coming to perfection, the failure of one thing repaired by the success of another....Though an old man, I am but a young gardener.

—Thomas Jefferson

You take life as it is and you don't complain. If there is a hereafter, I will be pleasantly surprised. When I was a little boy I wanted to see God. Moses had seen Him. I was a good little boy. I begged Him to come. He didn't and I think He was wrong.

I love life tremendously. I am an optimist. I think to myself, what will I do with my time?

—Arthur Rubinstein

Prescription for eternal youth:
Avoid fried meats, which angry up the blood.
If your stomach disputes you, lie down
    and pacify it with cool thoughts.
Keep the juices flowing by
    jangling gentle as you move.
Go very light on the vices,
    such as carrying on in society
        —the society ramble ain't restful.
Avoid running at all times.
And don't look back.
    Something might be gaining on you.

—Leroy "Satchel" Paige

Old age: the crown of life, our play's last act.
　　　　　　　—De Amicitia XXIII

The woods are lovely, dark and deep,
But I have promises to keep,
And miles to go before I sleep,
And miles to go before I sleep.

　　　　　　　—Robert Frost
　　　　　　　"Stopping by Woods on a
　　　　　　　　　Snowy Evening"

When an older person simply behaves like a healthy human being, he seems younger. Most older people play the role of being old.

　　　　　　　—Ashley Montagu

Action keeps the adrenalin flowing.

　　　　　　　—John Wayne

Live thy life,
　Young and old,
Like yon oak,
　Bright in spring,
　　Living gold.

　　　　　　　—Alfred, Lord Tennyson

It is always in season for old men to learn.

　　　　　　　—Aeschylus

We have no more right to consume happiness
　　without producing it
　　　than to consume wealth
　　　　without producing it.

　　　　　　　—George Bernard Shaw

I do not think the artist's meanings are nearly so important as the meanings his creations evoke in the spectators. As a matter of fact, these are the only meanings that count. They are the ones that make for the continuing life of a work of art, spreading its acceptance over generations of men.

　　　　　　　—Thomas Hart Benton

The life in us is like the water in the river. It may rise this year higher than man has ever known it, and flood the parched uplands; even this may be the eventful year.

—Henry David Thoreau

Don't you know me well enough to know I never close any doors? There are no absolutes in this world.

—Senator Everett Dirksen

Be glad of life because it gives you the chance to love and to work and to play and to look at the stars.

—Henry van Dyke

I'm too young to retire. Whoever heard of a thirty-nine-year-old man retiring. Why, I won't be forty until next year...or the year after that. Who knows?

—Jack Benny

Age is a state of mind. Success begins with good positive thoughts and goals:

1. Never look back. Yesterday is gone....*Look ahead!*
2. *Plan* each day with a *goal* to be achieved.
3. *Recognize disappointments* as challenges to make you stronger.
4. *Be realistic* in plans...but demand the best possible.
5. *Be honest* with yourself....Recognize the real you.
6. Always *"think young."*
7. Always *"think physically fit."*
8. Always *"think success."*
9. Always *"think I can...I can...I can."*
10. Remember...*"Miracles begin with you"*...be fair and you will go far.

—Jack LaLanne

My deepest feeling is one of hope. My hope is based on the fact of the universality of human beings, on the knowledge that the values they cherish most deeply are the same.

—Marian Anderson

DAVID MELTON

Every sunrise is a new message from God,
and every sunset His signature.

—William Arthur Ward

You do not know yet what it is to be 70 years old. I
will tell you, so that you may not be taken by
surprise when your turn comes. It is like climbing
the Alps. You reach a snow-crowned summit, and
see behind you the deep valley stretching miles and
miles away, and before you other summits higher
and whiter which you may have strength to climb or
may not. Then you sit down and meditate, and
wonder which it will be. That is the whole story,
amplify it as you may. All that one can say is, that
life is opportunity.

—Henry Wadsworth Longfellow

*Everyone enjoys feeling he can contribute. It is one
of the greatest feelings in the world—whether one
contributes to the family, community, or country.*

—Helen Brooke Taussig, M.D.

It's fun to grow old so long as you stay young, and I
will always be young at heart. Retire? Forget it. I
am 73 years old and still work 40 weeks a year. My
routine is demanding. I love it. It sure beats doing
needlepoint on the patio.

—Sally Rand

*I am neither stupid nor scared, and my sense of my
own importance to the world is relatively small. On
the other hand, my sense of my importance to myself
is tremendous. I am all I have, to work with, to play
with, to suffer and to enjoy. It is not the eyes of
others that I am wary of, but my own. I do not
intend to let myself down more than I can possibly
help, and I find that the fewer illusions that I have
about me or the world around me, the better
company I am for myself.*

—Noel Coward

*Keep working! Hard work never hurt anybody. More
people rest out than wear out.*

*. . . I'm eighty-six now, and making money when
you're my age is no different from making money
when you're younger; you just have to try harder.*

—Colonel Harland Sanders

In all ranks of life the human heart
yearns for the beautiful;
all the beautiful things that God makes
are his gift to all alike.

—Harriet Beecher Stowe

The grand essentials in this life are something to do, something to love, and something to hope for.

—Joseph Addison

God forbid that we should all mourn for the past. We have to go forward.

—Bette Davis

As long as you care the good Lord will smile down on you.

—Jesse Owen

I have written my life in small sketches, a little today, a little yesterday, as I thought of it, and as I remembered all the things from childhood on through the years, good ones, and unpleasant ones; that is how they come, and that is how we have to take them. I look back on my life like a good day's work; it was done and I feel satisfied with it. I was happy and contented, I knew nothing better and made the best out of what life offered. And life is what we make it, always has been, always will be.

—Grandma Moses

So it is quite clear: to love God, not myself; to do the will of God, not my own, and work for the good of others, not for my own, and all this always, everywhere and with great joy.

—Pope John XXIII

*I have asked
to be left a few tears
And some laughter.
. . . Time is a great teacher.*

—Carl Sandburg

I was an old man when I was 12; and now I am an old man, and it's splendid!

— *Thornton Wilder*

I like to think that I've helped to make people feel, in themselves, that they are working toward some better existence. I've had a very full, very rich life, with exciting work to do all the time, and a lovely happy life in the home, and if I've made people understand more about human beings by what I've done in the theatre, then, that will give me satisfaction. In fact, as the old miner said of <u>Medea</u>—"I would like to feel that I've kindled a fire."

— Dame Sybil Thorndike

I'm an old cupie,
Still full of whoopee.

— *Sophie Tucker*

In every man there is a divine spark, because every man is the son of God.

— Leo Tolstoy

. . .After my husband died, I was bored. . .unfulfilled. One night I was looking at television, and I saw, "Join the Peace Corps—Age No Barrier." I wrote that night for an application.

— Lillian Carter

. . .I believe that the welfare of each is bound up in the welfare of all. . . .I believe that life is given us so we may grow in love, and I believe that God is in me as the sun is in the colour and fragrance of a flower—the Light in my darkness, the Voice in my silence.

— Helen Keller

I've had some good young men working with me over the years, but only rarely do I see in them the same excitement of discovery I have felt so many times and still feel. I still have trouble taking time to answer my mail, because I'm fascinated by my work. I'm a theoretical man, so I never make a discovery by accident; it's an intellectual sort of excitement. If you can discover something new, it's important—even if you cannot see any immediate practical value in it. I wish more young people could feel that joy—the joy of discovery.

— *Linus Pauling*

. . .*I've spent my entire life in show business,. . .I didn't quit. I stayed in there, and I finally got so old that I became new again. I don't believe anybody should retire, no matter what his or her age is. In fact, that thought is so important I'm going to repeat it again—<u>I don't believe anybody should retire, no matter what his or her age is!</u> And I'm living proof of this point. Well, not completely living. I must admit that every Tuesday at five minutes after one, I cough a little.*

— *George Burns*

My life is the true story of an old man who still has the capacity to marvel at things and who wants to hold onto it until he breathes his last. I've always been . . . a man of energy and good will. I meet interesting people all the time, and some have become my friends. I'm evolving in a superior world where people accept me as I am: respectful, admiring and also humbly proud of my origins.

— *Maurice Chevalier*

Too much of a good thing is wonderful.

— Mae West

I am rich when a wrong is righted, and especially if I have contributed something to its doing. I am rich because of failures and lessons learned from them—because of dreams that failed to materialize and others that came true. Sensitivity to the needs of others can be the source of great happiness.

— Kate Smith

. . . we must avoid the impulse to live only for today, plundering, for our own ease and convenience, the precious resources of tomorrow.

— President Dwight D. Eisenhower

Look at life as though all your geese were swans and every swan a princess.

— Rosetta Smith

Let the meek inherit the earth—they have it coming to them.

— James Thurber

It is never too late to give up your prejudices.

— Henry David Thoreau

I have given my best, and I feel there is still more to give. This remains my purpose in life, to bring meaning to music each time I play. I am not tired of life. I can still feel wonder when it is a beautiful day.

— *Vladimir Horowitz*

Life takes courage. It takes believing in it. It takes work! It takes you liking me and me liking you. It takes the dreaming soul of the human race that wants it to go right. Whatever you do—never stop dreaming.

— *Ruth Gordon*

Life is suspended between two eternities—the time
to use it is today.

— Randall Guywehr

Minds that have nothing to confer
Find little to perceive.

— William Wordsworth

If I shoot at the sun, I may hit a star.

— P. T. Barnum

Each year is a new beginning . . .
a golden dawn on the horizon of life.

— Theresa Ann Hunt

To be of use in the world is the only way to be happy.
— Hans Christian Andersen

I did not know that I could scorn women at twenty and be
charmed by them at seventy.

— Auguste Rodin

Age appears to be best in four things — old wood,
best to burn, old wine to drink, old friends to trust,
and old authors to read.

— Sir Francis Bacon

I don't think retirement is a very good idea. . . . Man seeks
his own justification through work and feeling useful, so giving up the enormous personal satisfaction of being useful to
your fellow man is, I think, a mistake.

— Edward Durell Stone

To me every hour of the light and dark is a miracle.
Every cubic inch of space is a miracle.

—Walt Whitman

All my life I have felt privileged to have had good friends
around me, privileged to do the kinds of work I know and
love the best, and to have been born in a country whose
immense beauty and grandeur are matched only by the
greatness of her people.

— John Wayne

You and I have a rendezvous with destiny.
— President Ronald W. Reagan

How long should a person live? I don't know. What's more important is how you live and what you live for. As long as I have a breath of life I'm going to try to live actively and be a part of the daily life of my family and friends, my job, neighborhood, community and country.

—Hubert H. Humphrey

Employment is Nature's best physician, and is essential to human happiness.

—Galen, A.D. 172

Ideals are the best food for stamina.

—*Marlene Dietrich*

I am only a servant, that's all. I am a waiter—for God. We are all servants of God, or destiny, whatever you wish to call it. I am not so proud, and I am not so great—I'm nothing but what He has wanted me to be. He has said to me, "You are going to teach and serve and make them dance," and I know that nothing anybody on earth could do could prevent me from doing what He wants me to do.

—George Balanchine

Glory gives herself only to those who have dreamed of her....I belong to everyone and to no one....The man nobody knows...who became France.

The man of character stands erect, takes a firm position, and faces events.

—*Charles de Gaulle*

When I am alone with myself, I have not the courage to think of myself as an artist in the great and ancient sense of the term. Giotto, Titian, Rembrandt and Goya were great painters; I am only a public entertainer who has understood his times and has exhausted as best he could the imbecility, the vanity, the cupidity of his contemporaries. Mine is a bitter confession, more painful than it may appear, but it has the merit of being sincere.

—*Pablo Picasso*

Somebody once asked Picasso, "Of all the pictures you've done, which is your favorite?"

"The next one," Picasso replied.

I shall grow old, but never lose life's zest,
Because the road's last turn will be the best.

—Henry van Dyke

No person who is enthusiastic about his work has anything to fear from life.

—Samuel Goldwyn

In the central place of your heart is an evergreen tree.
Its name is love.
So long as it flourishes, you are young.

—Author Unknown

Only human values are life-giving values. No organic values are ever life-taking. When man builds "natural" buildings naturally, he builds his very life into them—inspired by intrinsic Nature in this interior sense we are here calling "organic."

—Frank Lloyd Wright

God is also my banker.
I may not have everything I want,
but I have everything I need.

—Ethel Waters

Do your duty and history will do you justice.

—Harry S. Truman

David Melton —author and illustrator

David Melton is one of the most versatile and prolific talents on the literary and art scenes today. His literary works span the gamut of factual prose, analytical essays, newsreporting, magazine articles, features, short stories, poetry and novels in both the adult and juvenile fields. When reviewing his credits, it is difficult to believe that such an outpouring of creative efforts came from just one person. In seventeen years, twenty-four of his books have been published, several of which have been translated into a number of languages.

Mr. Melton has illustrated ten of his own books and three by other authors, while many of his drawings and paintings have been reproduced as fine art prints, posters, puzzles, calendars, book jackets, record covers, mobiles and note cards, and they have been featured in national publications.

Mr. Melton has also gained wide reputation as a guest speaker and teacher. He has spoken to hundreds of professional, social and civic groups, relating the problems that confront parents and teachers of learning-disabled and handicapped children, and he has influenced the mandates of change in the field of special education and therapies for brain-injured children. He is also a frequent guest on local and national radio and television talk shows.

Since a number of Mr. Melton's books are enjoyed by children, he has visited hundreds of schools nationwide as a principal speaker in Author-in-Residence Programs, Young Authors' Days, and Children's Literature Festivals. He also conducts in-service seminars for teachers and teaches professional writing courses throughout the country.

To encourage and celebrate the creativity of students, Mr. Melton has developed the highly acclaimed teacher's manual, WRITTEN & ILLUSTRATED BY..., which is used in thousands of schools in teaching students to write and illustrate original books by *THE MELTON METHOD*. To provide opportunities for students to become professionally published authors and illustrators, in association with Landmark Editions, Inc., he helped initiate THE NATIONAL WRITTEN & ILLUSTRATED BY... AWARDS CONTEST FOR STUDENTS.

Author:

TODD
Prentice Hall — Softcover, Dell Publishing
New Edition — The Better Baby Press

WHEN CHILDREN NEED HELP
T. Y. Crowell — Softcover, Independence Press

CHILDREN OF DREAMS, CHILDREN OF HOPE
With Raymundo Veras, M.D.
Contemporary Books
New Edition — The Better Baby Press

A BOY CALLED HOPELESS
Softcover — Landmark Editions

THEODORE
Independence Press

SURVIVAL KIT FOR PARENTS OF TEENAGERS
St. Martin's Press

PROMISES TO KEEP
Franklin Watts

INDEPENDENCE —
The Queen City of the Trails
Landmark Editions

WRITTEN & ILLUSTRATED BY...
Landmark Editions, Inc.

Author and Illustrator:

I'LL SHOW YOU THE MORNING SUN
Stanyan-Random House

JUDY — A REMEMBRANCE
Stanyan-Random House

THIS MAN, JESUS
McGraw Hill

AND GOD CREATED...
Independence Press

HOW TO HELP YOUR PRESCHOOLER LEARN MORE, FASTER, AND BETTER
David McKay Co.

THE ONE AND ONLY AUTOBIOGRAPHY OF RALPH MILLER —
The Dog Who Knew He Was a Boy
Softcover — Landmark Editions

HARRY S. TRUMAN —
The Man Who Walked with Giants
Independence Press

THE ONE AND ONLY SECOND AUTOBIOGRAPHY OF RALPH MILLER —
The Dog Who Knew He Was a Boy
Softcover — Landmark Editions

HOW TO CAPTURE LIVE AUTHORS
and Bring Them to Your Schools
Softcover — Landmark Editions

Illustrator:

WHAT TO DO ABOUT YOUR BRAIN-INJURED CHILD
by Glenn Doman, Doubleday

GOOD-BYE MOMMY
by Bruce King Doman, The Better Baby Press
— Encyclopaedia Britannica

IMAGES OF GREATNESS
The Images of Greatness Commission

HOW TO BE YOUR OWN ASTROLOGER
by Sybil Leek, Cowles Book Co.

Designer:

HAPPY BIRTHDAY, AMERICA!
Independence Press